THE LITTLE BOOK OF

SHAKESPEARE ON LOVE

First published in 2024 by OH
An Imprint of HEADLINE PUBLISHING GROUP

2 4 6 8 10 9 7 5 3 1

Disclaimer:

Cataloguing in Publication Data is available from the British Library

ISBN 978-1-03541-978-4

Compiled and written by: Stella Caldwell
Editorial: Victoria Denne
Designed and typeset in Brioso Pro by: Tony Seddon
Project manager: Russell Porter
Production: Marion Storz
Printed and bound in China

HEADLINE PUBLISHING GROUP
An Hachette UK Company
Carmelite House, 50 Victoria Embankment, London EC4Y 0DZ

www.headline.co.uk   www.hachette.co.uk

THE LITTLE BOOK OF
SHAKESPEARE ON LOVE

THE BARD'S MOST ROMANTIC LINES

CONTENTS

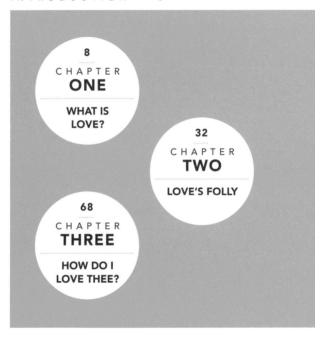

INTRODUCTION

No writer, before or since, has matched Shakespeare in terms of influence, critical acclaim or popular success. And the Bard had plenty to say about the subject of love – the word appears more than 2,000 times in his collected works!

Love weaves its way through Shakespeare's writing with extraordinary beauty and depth. From the tumultuous passion of star-crossed lovers to the steadfast bonds of family and friendship, the writer's insights into the workings of the human heart continue to resonate today.

In *Romeo and Juliet*, love is depicted as a powerful and all-consuming force that transcends familial feuds but ultimately leads to tragic consequences. In *Othello*, it is tainted by jealousy and mistrust, leading to devastating outcomes. And in the romantic comedies, such as *Much Ado About Nothing* or *Twelfth Night*, love transcends social barriers and conventions. While there may be obstacles and challenges – unfaithful lovers, scheming deceivers and mistaken identities – these plays celebrate love's power to unite and transform lives.

But, for Shakespeare, love is not confined to the romantic type. Whether it be the destructive passion between Antony and Cleopatra, the enduring friendship of Hamlet and Horatio or the poignant bond between Prospero and his daughter, Miranda, the dramatist explores love in all its guises – and evokes its joys, triumphs, perils and sorrows with unflinching honesty. From the intoxicating allure of first love to the heart-wrenching pain of betrayal and loss, Shakespeare captures the full spectrum of human experience.

This Little Book is a delightful collection of timeless quotes. Complemented by fascinating insights into the Bard's life and works, it's a celebration of his enduring legacy as a poet of the heart – and contains some of the most romantic and profound lines ever written in the English language.

1

WHAT IS LOVE?

Love is a multifaceted theme in Shakespeare's works. It embodies passion in *Romeo and Juliet*, lighthearted silliness in *A Midsummer Night's Dream* and jealousy in *Othello*. A force of nature, love is capable of inspiring greatness and destruction alike, and reflects the complexities and contradictions inherent in human relationships.

If you include the words "loved", "beloved" and "loving", the word "love" appears 2,338 times in Shakespeare's collected works.

What is love? 'tis not hereafter;

Present mirth hath present laughter;

What's to come is still unsure:

In delay there lies no plenty –

Then come kiss me, Sweet-and-twenty,

Youth's a stuff will not endure.

The Clown
Twelfth Night, Act 2, Scene 3

Why then, O brawling love, O loving hate,

O anything of nothing first create!

O heavy lightness, serious vanity,

Misshapen chaos of well-seeming forms!

Feather of lead, bright smoke,
cold fire, sick health,

Still-waking sleep that is not what it is!

Romeo
Romeo and Juliet, Act 1, Scene 1

Loving goes by haps;

Some Cupid kills with arrows,

some with traps.

Hero

Much Ado About Nothing, Act 3, Scene 2

Shakespeare's 154 sonnets explore various aspects of love, including its fleeting nature, its power, and its ability to inspire and torment. Characterized by their emotional depth and intricate wordplay, these poems are considered some of the most beautiful and profound expressions of love in the English language.

Love is not love

Which alters when it alteration finds,

Or bends with the remover to remove:

O no! it is an ever-fixed mark

That looks on tempests and is never shaken.

Sonnet 116

A lover's eyes will gaze an eagle blind.

A lover's ear will hear the lowest sound,

When the suspicious head of
theft is stopped.

Love's feeling is more soft and sensible

Than are the tender horns of
cockled snails.

Berowne
Love's Labour's Lost, Act 4, Scene 3

Love goes toward love as schoolboys
from their books,

But love from love, toward school
with heavy looks.

Romeo
Romeo and Juliet, Act 2, Scene 2

Many of Shakespeare's most famous plays revolve around the theme of love. Some, such as *A Midsummer Night's Dream* and *Much Ado About Nothing* are romantic comedies. Others, such as *Hamlet* or *Antony and Cleopatra*, explore the complexities, tragedy and pain that all too often accompany this emotion.

Love looks not with the eyes,
but with the mind,

And therefore is winged Cupid
painted blind.

Helena
A Midsummer Night's Dream, **Act 1, Scene 1**

Love is like a child,

That longs for everything it can come by.

Duke

The Two Gentlemen of Verona, Act 3, Scene 1

There's beggary in the love
that can be reckoned.

Antony
Antony and Cleopatra, **Act 1, Scene 1**

Love comforteth like sunshine after rain,
But Lust's effect is tempest after sun;
Love's gentle spring doth always fresh remain;
Lust's winter comes ere summer half be done;
Love surfeits not, Lust like a glutton dies;
Love is all truth, Lust full of forgèd lies.

Venus and Adonis

But love, first learnèd in a lady's eyes,

Lives not alone immurèd in the brain,

But with the motion of all elements

Courses as swift as thought in every power,

And gives to every power a double power,

Above their functions and their offices.

Berowne
Love's Labour Lost, Act 4, Scene 3

Shakespeare's sonnets generally
follow a specific form, consisting of
14 lines written in iambic pentameter.
Each line has 10 syllables with a stress
on every second syllable, and the sonnet
is structured into three quatrains (four-
line stanzas) and a concluding couplet
(a two-line stanza).

My love is as a fever, longing still
For that which longer nurseth the disease,
Feeding on that which doth preserve the ill,
Th' uncertain sickly appetite to please.

Sonnet 147

And when love speaks, the voice
of all the gods

Make heaven drowsy with the harmony.

Berowne
Love's Labour's Lost, Act 4, Scene 3

Jack shall have Jill,

Nought shall go ill,

The man shall have his mare again,
and all shall be well.

Puck
A Midsummer Night's Dream, Act 3, Scene 2

Do thou but close our hands
with holy words,

Then love-devouring death
do what he dare;

It is enough I may but call her mine.

Romeo
Romeo and Juliet, Act 2, Scene 6

Love is a familiar. Love is a devil.

There is no evil angel but love.

Don Adriano de Armado
Love's Labour Lost, Act 1, Scene 2

She loved me for the dangers I had passed,

And I loved her that she did pity them.

Othello
Othello, Act 1, Scene 3

For thy sweet love remembered such wealth brings,

That then I scorn to change my state with kings.

Sonnet 29

2

LOVE'S FOLLY

"The course of true love never did run smooth," reflects Lysander in *A Midsummer Night's Dream*. Indeed, Shakespeare's characters are often consumed with irrational fervour – love, with its intensity and unpredictability, can push individuals to a place where the line between reason and folly is blurred.

At the age of 18, Shakespeare married
26-year-old Anne Hathaway – who was
already pregnant with their first child.
The marriage was considered highly
unusual, as Shakespeare was significantly
younger than Anne. Their marriage
resulted in three children: Susanna,
Judith and Hamnet.

The course of true love never did run smooth.

Lysander
A Midsummer Night's Dream, Act 1, Scene 1

You have witchcraft in your lips, Kate.

King Henry
Henry V, Act 5, Scene 2

If thou rememb'rest not the slightest folly

That ever love did make thee run into,

Thou has not loved.

Silvius

As You Like It, Act 2, Scene 4

That's a deep story of a deeper love,

For he was more than over shoes in love.

Proteus

The Two Gentlemen of Verona, Act 1, Scene 1

O, swear not by the moon,
th' inconstant moon,

That monthly changes in her circled orb,

Lest that thy love prove likewise variable.

Juliet
Romeo and Juliet, Act 2, Scene 2

Love is a smoke raised with the fume of sighs;

Being purged, a fire sparkling in lovers' eyes;

Being vexed, a sea nourished with lovers' tears:

What is it else? A madness most discreet,

A choking gall, and a preserving sweet.

Romeo
Romeo and Juliet, Act 1, Scene 1

O, how this spring of love resembleth
The uncertain glory of an April day,
Which now shows all the beauty of the sun,
And by and by a cloud takes all away!

Proteus
The Two Gentlemen of Verona, Act 1, Scene 3

Shakespeare famously left his wife, Anne, his "second-best bed" in his will. While it might be seen as a snub, some researchers believe it was a gift from the heart. The best bed was typically kept in the guest room, and so the second-best bed was the marital bed – where William and Anne would have slept together, and where their children were born.

Item I gyve unto my wife my second-best
bed with the furniture.

From the will of William Shakespeare,
25 March 1616

I'll follow thee and make a heaven of hell,

To die upon the hand I love so well.

Helena
A Midsummer Night's Dream, Act 2, Scene 1

If music be the food of love, play on.

Give me excess of it, that, surfeiting,

The appetite may sicken and so die.

Duke Orsino
Twelfth Night, Act 1, Scene 1

I am too sore empiercèd with his shaft

To soar with his light feathers,
and so bound,

I cannot bound a pitch above dull woe;

Under love's heavy burden do I sink.

Romeo
Romeo and Juliet, Act 1, Scene 4

Love is merely a madness, and,
I tell you, deserves

as well a dark house and a whip as
madmen do;

and the reason why they are not so
punished and cured

is that the lunacy is so ordinary
that the whippers

are in love too.

Rosalind
As You Like It, Act 3, Scene 2

Cupid is a knavish lad, thus to
make poor females mad.

Puck
A Midsummer Night's Dream, Act 3, Scene 2

Good night, good night!

Parting is such sweet sorrow,

That I shall say good night till it be morrow.

Juliet
Romeo and Juliet, **Act 2, Scene 2**

Shakespeare's love stories often push the boundaries of traditional romance. Examples include the passionate and tragic love between Othello and Desdemona in *Othello*, and the transformative love between Prospero and his daughter, Miranda, in *The Tempest*.

I kissed thee ere I killed thee,
no way but this,

Killing myself, to die upon a kiss.

Othello
Othello, Act 5, Scene 2

They do not love that do not
show their love.

Julia
The Two Gentlemen of Verona, Act 1, Scene 2

What light is light, if Silvia be not seen?

What joy is joy, if Silvia be not by?

Valentine

The Two Gentlemen of Verona, Act 3, Scene 1

The barge she sat in, like a burnished throne,

Burned on the water: the poop was beaten gold;

Purple the sails, and so perfumed that

The winds were lovesick with them;
the oars were silver,

Which to the tune of flutes kept stroke, and made

The water which they beat to follow faster,

As amorous of their strokes.

Enobarbus
Antony and Cleopatra, Act 2, Scene 2

Sigh no more, ladies, sigh no more,

Men were deceivers ever,

One foot in sea, and one on shore,

To one thing constant never.

Balthasar
Much Ado About Nothing, Act 2, Scene 3

One of the first reviews of *A Midsummer Night's Dream* was recorded by Samuel Pepys, who saw the play performed in 1662. In his famous diary he wrote that it was "the most insipid, ridiculous play that ever I saw in my life" – though he added that he enjoyed the dancing, as well as the "handsome women" he saw!

O Helena, goddess, nymph, perfect, divine!

Demetrius
A Midsummer Night's Dream, Act 3, Scene 2

Alas that love whose view is muffled still,

Should without eyes see pathways to his will.

Romeo
Romeo and Juliet, Act 1, Scene 1

Things base and vile, holding no quantity,

Love can transpose to form and dignity.

Helena
A Midsummer Night's Dream, Act 1, Scene 1

When you depart from me,

sorrow abides and happiness
takes his leave.

Leonato
Much Ado About Nothing, Act 1, Scene 1

Suffer love! A good epithet!

I do suffer love indeed,

For I love thee against my will.

Benedick
Much Ado About Nothing, Act 5, Scene 2

This is the very ecstasy of love,

Whose violent property fordoes itself

And leads the will to desperate undertakings

As oft as any passion under heaven

That does afflict our natures.

Polonius
Hamlet, Act 2, Scene 1

This love feel I, that feel no love in this.

Romeo
Romeo and Juliet, **Act 1, Scene 1**

Alas, that love, so gentle in his view,

Should be so tyrannous and rough
in proof!

Romeo
Romeo and Juliet, Act 1, Scene 1

O, withered is the garland of the war,

The soldier's pole is fall'n: young boys and girls

Are level now with men; the odds is gone,

And there is nothing left remarkable

Beneath the visiting moon.

Cleopatra
Antony and Cleopatra, Act 4, Scene 15

My love to love is love but to disgrace it,

For I have heard it is a life in death,

That laughs and weeps, and all but
with a breath.

Venus and Adonis

And I pray thee now tell me,

For which of my bad parts didst thou first
fall in love with me?

Benedick
Much Ado About Nothing, Act 5, Scene 2

3

HOW DO I LOVE THEE?

From the tumultuous passion of
Romeo and Juliet to the "merry war"
between Beatrice and Benedick,
declarations of love resound with
eloquence and grace in Shakespeare's
works. Across genres and characters,
the dramatist masterfully navigates the
complexities of the heart, revealing
its power to transform, unite and
ultimately define the human experience.

My bounty is as boundless as the sea,

My love as deep. The more I give to thee,

The more I have, for both are infinite.

Juliet
Romeo and Juliet, **Act 2, Scene 2**

I would not wish any companion
in the world but you;

Nor can imagination form a shape,

Besides yourself, to like of.

Miranda
The Tempest, Act 3, Scene 1

Written in 1609 and undoubtedly the
best known of Shakespeare's 154 sonnets,
"Shall I compare thee to a summer's day?"
– or Sonnet 18 – touches on the themes
of unattainable love and mortality.
The poem is part of Shakespeare's "Fair
Youth" sequence of sonnets, which many
historians believe are addressed to a
young man.

Shall I compare thee to a summer's day?

Thou art more lovely and more temperate.

Sonnet 18

So are you to my thoughts as food to life,

Or as sweet-seasoned showers are
to the ground...

Sonnet 75

Cesario, by the roses of the spring,

By maidhood, honour, truth, and everything,

I love thee so.

Olivia
Twelfth Night, **Act 3, Scene 1**

O my dear lord,

I crave no other nor no better man.

Mariana
Measure for Measure, Act 5, Scene 1

Those lines that I before have writ do lie,

Ev'n those that said I could not love you dearer.

Yet then my judgment knew no reason why

My most full flame should afterwards burn clearer.

Sonnet 115

Love Duos

From the witty love banter in *Much Ado About Nothing* to the jealousy and betrayal at the heart of *Othello*, the couples in Shakespeare's works embody the complexities and joys of human relationships.

Here are 10 famous pairings:

Beatrice and Benedick –
Much Ado About Nothing

Hotspur and Lady Percy – *Henry IV, Part 1*

Viola and Orsino – *Twelfth Night*

Florizel and Perdita – *The Winter's Tale*

Berowne and Rosaline –
Love's Labour's Lost

Macbeth and Lady Macbeth – *Macbeth*

Desdemona and Othello – *Othello*

Antony and Cleopatra –
Antony and Cleopatra

Bertram and Helena –
All's Well That Ends Well

Ferdinand and Miranda –
The Tempest

What's mine is yours and
what is yours is mine.

Duke

Measure for Measure, Act 5, Scene 1

This bud of love by summer's ripening breath,

May prove a beauteous flower when next we meet.

Juliet
Romeo and Juliet, Act 2, Scene 2

Not marble nor the gilded monuments

Of princes, shall outlive this
powerful rhyme,

But you shall shine more bright
in these contents

Than unswept stone, besmeared
with sluttish time.

Sonnet 55

O, how thy worth with manners may I sing,

When thou art all the better part of me?

Sonnet 39

You lie, in faith; for you are call'd plain Kate,

And bonny Kate and sometimes Kate the curst;

But Kate, the prettiest Kate in Christendom,

Kate of Kate Hall, my super-dainty Kate,

For dainties are all Kates, and therefore, Kate,

Take this of me, Kate of my consolation…

Hearing thy mildness praised in every town,
Thy virtues spoke of, and thy beauty sounded,
Yet not so deeply as to thee belongs,
Myself am moved to woo thee for my wife.

Petruchio
The Taming of the Shrew, Act 2, Scene 1

What is your substance, whereof are
you made,

That millions of strange shadows on
you tend?

Since every one hath, every one, one shade,

And you but one, can every shadow lend.

Sonnet 53

Why, there's a wench! Come on,
and kiss me, Kate.

Petruchio
The Taming of the Shrew, Act 5, Scene 2

A Midsummer Night's Dream is one of Shakespeare's most popular and frequently performed plays. With its whimsical and fantastical elements – including fairies, love potions and mistaken identities – the play has inspired numerous adaptations, films and even ballets.

My love, my life, my soul, fair Helena!

Lysander
A Midsummer Night's Dream, **Act 3, Scene 2**

Nor did I wonder at the lily's white,

Nor praise the deep vermilion in the rose;

They were but sweet, but figures of delight,

Drawn after you, you pattern of all those.

Sonnet 98

I will not be sworn but love may
transform me to an oyster.

Benedick
Much Ado About Nothing, Act 2, Scene 3

Hear my soul speak. Of the very
instant that I saw you,

Did my heart fly at your service.

Ferdinand
The Tempest, Act 3, Scene 1

I do love nothing in the world so well as you.

Benedick
Much Ado About Nothing, Act 4, Scene 1

Thee will I love, and with thee lead my life.

Antipholus of Syracuse
The Comedy of Errors, Act 3, Scene 2

When you do dance, I wish you
A wave o' th' sea, that you might ever do
Nothing but that...

Florizel
The Winter's Tale, Act 4, Scene 4

Elizabethans sometimes referred to the female anatomy as "nothing" or "no-thing", which gives Shakespeare's *Much Ado About Nothing* another level of suggestive meaning.

"

I love you with so much of my heart
that none is left to protest.

"

Beatrice
Much Ado About Nothing, **Act 4, Scene 1**

I will live in thy heart, die in thy lap,
and be buried in thy eyes.

Benedick
Much Ado About Nothing, Act 5, Scene 2

I know no ways to mince it in love,

but directly to say, 'I love you'.

King Henry
Henry V, Act 5, Scene 2

By my troth, I kiss thee with a most
constant heart.

Doll Tearsheet
Henry IV, Part 2, Act 2, Scene 4

A heaven on earth I have won by wooing thee.

Bertram

All's Well That Ends Well, Act 4, Scene 2

4

LOVE'S FLAME

Whether love's flame burns brightly or consumes with destructive fury, it can be a powerful tide that sweeps souls into its embrace. From the smouldering desire of *Antony and Cleopatra* to the fervent declarations of *Romeo and Juliet*, Shakespeare presents love as a powerful force of nature – passionate, romantic and heady.

With love's light wings did I o'erperch
these walls,

For stony limits cannot hold love out...

And what love can do, that dares
love attempt.

Therefore thy kinsmen are no stop to me.

Romeo
Romeo and Juliet, Act 2, Scene 2

Doubt that the stars are fire,

Doubt that the sun doth move,

Doubt truth to be a liar,

But never doubt I love.

Hamlet
Hamlet, Act 2, Scene 2

No one has shaped the modern rom-com genre as much as Shakespeare. Perhaps the Bard's most influential romantic comedy is *Much Ado About Nothing*, the timeless tale of sworn enemies who become lovers. Countless pop-culture pairings owe a debt to the play, from Elizabeth and Mr Darcy in *Pride and Prejudice* to the leads in *When Harry Met Sally* and *Something's Gotta Give*.

I thank God and my cold blood I am of your humour for that.

I had rather hear my dog bark at a crow than a man swear he loves me.

Beatrice
Much Ado About Nothing, Act 1, Scene 1

She's beautiful, and therefore to be wooed;

She is woman, and therefore to be won.

Suffolk

Henry VI, Part 1, Act 5, Scene 3

But soft, what light through yonder window breaks?

It is the east, and Juliet is the sun.

Romeo
Romeo and Juliet, Act 2, Scene 2

The sight of lovers feedeth those in love.

Rosalind

As You Like It, Act 3, Scene 4

Now, for the love of Love and her soft hours,

Let's not confound the time with conference harsh.

There's not a minute of our lives should stretch

Without some pleasure now. What sport tonight?

Antony

Antony and Cleopatra, Act 1, Scene 1

Come what sorrow can,

It cannot countervail the exchange of joy,

That one short minute gives me in her sight.

Romeo
Romeo and Juliet, Act 2, Scene 6

Her passions are made of nothing
but the finest part of pure love.

Enobarbus
Anotony and Cleopatra, Act 1, Scene 2

Rosalind: "Now tell me how long you would have her after you have possessed her."

Orlando: "For ever and a day."

As You Like It, **Act 4, Scene 1**

Hero thinks surely she will die, for she
says she will die if he love her not,

And she will die ere she might
make her love known.

Claudio
Much Ado About Nothing, Act 2, Scene 3

Her bed is India: there she lies, a pearl.

Troilus
Troilus and Cressida, Act 1, Scene 1

O, wilt thou leave me so unsatisfied?

Romeo
Romeo and Juliet, Act 2, Scene 2

Shakespeare's story of the star-crossed lovers Romeo and Juliet is perhaps his most romantic play. Ninety per cent of the play is in verse and contains some of the Bard's loveliest poetry – including the beautiful sonnet Romeo and Juliet share when they first meet.

If I profane with my unworthiest hand

This holy shrine, the gentle sin is this:

My lips, two blushing pilgrims, ready stand

To smooth that rough touch with
a tender kiss.

Romeo
Romeo and Juliet, **Act 1, Scene 5**

So is mine eye enthrallèd to thy shape.

Titania
A Midsummer Night's Dream, Act 3, Scene 1

Beshrew your eyes,

They have o'erlooked me and divided me.

One half of me is yours, the other half yours –

Mine own, I would say. But if mine, then yours,

And so all yours.

Portia
The Merchant of Venice, **Act 3, Scene 2**

That on the touching of her lips I may

Melt and no more be seen.
O, come, be buried

A second time within these arms...

Pericles
Pericles, Act 5, Scene 3

He eats nothing but doves, love, and that breeds hot blood, and hot blood begets hot thoughts, and hot thoughts beget hot deeds, and hot deeds is love.

Paris

Troilus and Cressida, Act 3, Scene 1

Age cannot wither her, not custom stale

Her infinite variety.

Enobarbus
Antony and Cleopatra, Act 2, Scene 2

Did my heart love till now?

Forswear it, sight!

For I ne'er saw true beauty till this night.

Romeo
Romeo and Juliet, Act 1, Scene 5

You are a lover. Borrow Cupid's wings

And soar with them above a common bound.

Mercutio
Romeo and Juliet, Act 1, Scene 4

See how she leans her cheek upon her hand,

O that I were a glove upon that hand
that I might touch that cheek!

Romeo
Romeo and Juliet, Act 2, Scene 2

Lovers can see to do their amorous rites
By their own beauties; or, if love be blind,
It best agrees with night.

Juliet
Romeo and Juliet, Act 3, Scene 2

Journeys end in lovers meeting,

Every wise man's son doth know.

Fool
Twelfth Night, Act 2, Scene 3

Hamlet, a tragic tale of revenge, madness and love, is Shakespeare's longest play – while the character of Hamlet has more lines than any other Shakespearean character. The drama is celebrated for the number of phrases that have passed into everyday speech. As well as the line opposite, they include "to the manner born", "cruel to be kind" and "brevity is the soul of wit".

The lady doth protest too much, methinks.

Gertrude
Hamlet, Act 3, Scene 2

I loved Ophelia: Forty thousand brothers

Could not, with all their quantity of love,

Make up my sum.

Hamlet

Hamlet, Act 5, Scene 1

Where love is great, the littlest
doubts are fear.

Where little fears grow great,
great love grows there.

Player Queen
Hamlet, Act 3, Scene 2

O, she doth teach the torches to burn bright!

It seems she hangs upon the cheek of night

As a rich jewel in an Ethiop's ear –

Beauty too rich for use, for Earth too dear!

Romeo

Romeo and Juliet, **Act 1, Scene 5**

O heaven, O earth, bear witness to this sound
And crown what I profess with kind event
If I speak true! If hollowly, invert
What best is boded me to mischief! I
Beyond all limit of what else i' th' world
Do love, prize, honour you.

Ferdinand
The Tempest, Act 3, Scene 1

Eternity was in our lips and in our eyes.

Cleopatra
Antony and Cleopatra, Act 1, Scene 3

Egypt, thou knew'st too well

My heart was to thy rudder tied
by th'strings

And thou shouldst tow me after.

Antony
Antony and Cleopatra, Act 3, Scene 11

Silence is the perfectest herald of joy.

I were but little happy if I could
say how much.

Lady, as you are mine, I am yours.

I give away myself for you and
dote upon the exchange.

Claudio
Much Ado About Nothing, Act 2, Scene 1

I'll be a park, and thou shalt be my deer;

Feed where thou wilt, on mountain or in dale:

Graze on my lips, and if those hills be dry,

Stray lower, where the pleasant fountains lie.

Venus and Adonis

Romeo and Juliet has had quite an effect on the English language, popularizing words and phrases such as "ladybird" and "wild goose chase", while "Romeo" has become shorthand for a male lover.

Nay, if our wits run the wild goose chase,
I am done;

for thou hast more of the wild goose
in one of thy wits than,

I am sure, I have in my whole five –

Was I with you there for the goose?

Mercutio
Romeo and Juliet, Act 2, Scene 4

5

KINSHIP

The themes of friendship and familial love are intricately woven into the fabric of Shakespeare's works. In *Hamlet*, the unwavering bond between Hamlet and Horatio serves as a beacon of loyalty amidst betrayal and deceit, while in *King Lear*, the poignant relationship between Lear and his daughters epitomizes both the depth of paternal love and the consequences of familial discord.

Not that I think you did not love your father

But that I know love is begun by time,

And that I see, in passages of proof,

Time qualifies the spark and fire of it.

Claudius
Hamlet, Act 4, Scene 7

But if the while I think on thee, dear friend,

All losses are restored and sorrows end.

Sonnet 30

I desire you in friendship,

and I will one way or other make you amends.

Doctor Caius
The Merry Wives of Windsor, Act 3, Scene 1

So we grew together,

Like to a double cherry: seeming parted,

But yet an union in partition,

Two lovely berries moulded on one stem.

Helena
A Midsummer Night's Dream, **Act 3, Scene 2**

I love your majesty

According to my bond, no more nor less.

Cordelia
King Lear, Act 1, Scene 1

I count myself in nothing else so happy

As in a soul remembering my good friends;

And as my fortune ripens with thy love,

It shall be still thy true love's recompense.

My heart this covenant makes my hand
thus seals it.

Henry Bolingbroke
Richard II, Act 2, Scene 3

Shakespeare wasn't the first author to write about the Montagues and the Capulets, the two families at the centre of the rivalry that makes Romeo and Juliet's romance an impossible predicament. Italian poet Dante refers to them in his epic poem, *Divine Comedy*, written at the beginning of the 14th century.

My only love sprung from my only hate!

Too early seen unknown, and known too late!

Juliet
Romeo and Juliet, Act 1, Scene 5

Friendship is constant in all other things,

save in the office and affairs of love.

Claudio
Much Ado About Nothing, Act 2, Scene 1

Keep thy friend, under thy own life's key.

Countess of Roussillon

All's Well That Ends Well, Act 1, Scene 1

Male jealousy is a recurring theme
in works such as *Troilus and Cressida,*
Much Ado About Nothing, Cymbeline,
The Winter's Tale and *Othello.*
These plays highlight the dangers of
what *Othello*'s Iago famously calls the
"green-eyed monster" and its potential to
unravel relationships and lives.

O beware, my lord, of jealousy;

It is the green-eyed monster which doth
mock the meat it feeds on.

Iago
Othello, Act 3, Scene 3

Those friends thou hast, and their adoption tried,

Grapple them unto thy soul with hoops of steel.

Polonius
Hamlet, Act 1, Scene 3

To me, fair friend, you never can be old,

For as you were when first your eye I eyed,

Such seems your beauty still.

Sonnet 104

A friend should bear his
friend's infirmities.

Cassius

Julius Caesar, Act 4, Scene 3

The law of friendship bids me to conceal...

Proteus

The Two Gentlemen of Verona, Act 3, Scene 1

Ceremony was but devised at first

To set a gloss on faint deeds,
hollow welcomes,

Recanting goodness, sorry ere 'tis shown;

But where there is true friendship,
there needs none.

Timon
Timon of Athens, Act 1, Scene 2

My king, my Jove! I speak to thee, my heart!

Falstaff
Henry IV, Part 2, Act 5, Scene 5

To mingle friendship far is mingling
bloods.

Leontes

The Winter's Tale, Act 1, Scene 2

Thy friendship makes us fresh.

Charles

Henry VI, Part 1, Act 3, Scene 3

The theme of family love is prominently explored in *King Lear.* The play revolves around the tragic story of the king and his three daughters, examining themes of loyalty, betrayal and the consequences of misguided love.

Sir, I do love you more than words can wield the matter,

Dearer than eyesight, space, and liberty,

Beyond what can be valued, rich or rare,

No less than life, with grace, health, beauty, honour,

As much as child e'er loved or father found –

A love that makes breath poor and speech unable.

Beyond all manner of so much I love you.

Goneril
King Lear, Act 1, Scene 1

Thy sting is not so sharp

As friend remembered not...

Most friendship is feigning,
most loving mere folly.

Lord Amiens
As You Like It, Act 2, Scene 7

Love's not love

When it is mingled with regards that stand

Aloof from the entire point.

The King of France
King Lear, Act 1, Scene 1

6

WISE
COUNSEL

Four hundred years may have
passed since Shakespeare's death, but
his extraordinary insights into human
nature continue to resonate today. The
Bard ran the gamut of human experience
in his works, reflecting on love's joys and
sorrows and skillfully crafting words into
profound nuggets of wisdom.

Love moderately; long love doth so.

Too swift arrives as tardy as too slow.

Friar Laurence
Romeo and Juliet, Act 2, Scene 6

For lovers ever run before the clock.

Gratiano
The Merchant of Venice, Act 2, Scene 6

And yet, to say the truth,

Reason and love keep little company
together nowadays.

Bottom

A Midsummer Night's Dream, Act 3, Scene 1

Speak low if you speak love.

Don Pedro

Much Ado About Nothing, Act 2, Scene 1

Shakespeare often explored love crossing societal boundaries, challenging conventions of class, age and even gender. In *Twelfth Night*, for example, the character Viola disguises herself as a man, leading to a complex web of love interests and mistaken identities.

Conceal me what I am, and be my aid
For such disguise as haply shall become
The form of my intent. I'll serve this duke.
Thou shalt present me as an eunuch to him.

Viola
Twelfth Night, Act 1, Scene 2

Who ever loved that loved not at first sight?

Phoebe

As You Like It, Act 3, Scene 5

(Shakespeare was in fact quoting from
Christopher Marlowe's *Hero and Leander*)

O love, be moderate. Allay thy ecstasy.

In measure rein thy joy. Scant this excess.

I feel too much thy blessing. Make it less,

For fear I surfeit.

Portia
The Merchant of Venice, Act 3, Scene 2

Much Ado About Nothing
features more prose, or
unstructured text, than nearly
any other Shakespearean play,
with only 25 per cent of the play
in verse. Only *The Winter's Tale*
contains more prose.

Therefore all hearts in love use
their own tongues.

Let every eye negotiate for itself

And trust no agent, for beauty is a witch

Against whose charms faith melteth
into blood.

Much Ado About Nothing, Act 2, Scene 1

They say all lovers swear more
performance than they are able and yet
reserve an ability that they never perform,
vowing more than the perfection often and
discharging less than the tenth part of one.

Cressida
Troilus and Cressida, Act 3, Scene 2

And yet, by heaven, I think my love as rare

As any she belied with false compare.

Sonnet 130

The Oscar-winning *Shakespeare in Love*
tells the fictionalized story of the young
playwright struggling with writer's block.
Through a chance encounter, he falls in
love with a woman who becomes his muse
and inspires the creation of the Bard's most
famous love story, *Romeo and Juliet*. The film
also references *Hamlet*, *Twelfth Night* and
Shakespeare's most famous sonnet, Sonnet 18.

If love be blind, love cannot hit the mark.

Mercutio
Romeo and Juliet, Act 2, Scene 1

In Shakespeare's time and up until 1660, all stage roles were performed by men. It wasn't until 1662 that an actress stepped onto the stage as Juliet – Mary Saunderson is believed to be the first woman to play the iconic role.

What's in a name? That which we call a rose
By any other word would smell as sweet.

Juliet
Romeo and Juliet, **Act 2, Scene 2**

Men's vows are women's traitors.

Imogen
Cymbeline, Act 3, Scene 4

I pray you, do not fall in love with me,

For I am falser than vows made in wine.

Rosalind

As You Like It, Act 3, Scene 5

The Tempest, written in 1610–11, is widely thought to be the last play that Shakespeare wrote alone. The drama showcases many kinds of love, from the lover's bond between Ferdinand and Miranda to the family love shared by Prospero and Miranda or between Alonso and Ferdinand. Then there is the love for one's home – Prospero, Antonio and Alonso for their kingdoms, and Caliban for the magical island.

I am your wife, if you will marry me.
If not, I'll die your maid. To be your fellow
You may deny me, but I'll be your servant
Whether you will or no.

Miranda
The Tempest, Act 3, Scene 1

Young men's love then lies

Not truly in their hearts

but in their eyes.

Friar Lawrence
Romeo and Juliet, Act 2, Scene 3

Love sought is good, but given
unsought is better.

Olivia
Twelfth Night, Act 3, Scene 1

Love alters not with his brief hours and weeks,

But bears it out even to the edge of doom.

If this be error and upon me proved,

I never writ, nor no man ever loved.

Sonnet 116